How to see the World

in a

Weekend

Christine Krzyszton

Christine Krzyszton

Dedication

When I declare that I'm not going to be home this weekend, there are three people who are more than understanding: my son, and my dear sisters. I thank them for that and realize I could not have written this book if they were not so supportive. My friends Geoff and Karyn are supportive for a different reason, they travel with me, so thanks to them for making my travels more interesting and for their willingness to see the world in a weekend with me.

Thanks also to Kim Weiss for editing some of my content and removing 90% of my semi-colons.

Table of Contents

World in a Weekend Trip reports

Forward by Rick Ingersoll, the Frugal Travel Guy

A simple Google search changed my life about 12 years ago. I'd just seen a guy pay his bar tab with a Northwest Airlines Visa credit card and asked him what using that credit card got him. The ensuing Googling of the term "free frequent flyer miles" and the wonderful world of discount travel I found online has led my wife Katy and I on an eye opening and affordable adventure around the world. Twice, in fact, on Around the World itineraries and too many side trips to count, we have had the opportunity, the privilege, to visit 64 countries to date. All at prices we could afford.

What we found was a community of like-minded people with the desire to travel and either the financial restraints that prevented them for doing so, or folks like me, just too cheap to pay retail prices for travel. This underground community had found, and was sharing the secrets of discounted travel. They were sharing the secrets and as a group we were all benefiting from the experience of others.

My extended family lived on a website and forum called Flyertalk. When I joined in July of 2001 there were 15,000 members. Today the number has grown to over 400,000.

In October of 2007, after becoming the "travel expert" for my friends and acquaintances for the last 6 years, I came upon a USA Today article that described how a gal had started a blog sharing her recipe secrets and was actually monetizing the blog with advertising. I had found my vehicle to spread the word and the Frugal Travel Guy blog began. My goal was to condense and return back to the beginners in the hobby all I had learned in the past 6 years. My blog was sold to the owners of Flyertalk in January of 2012. I still try to spread the message as others did before me. This community is all about the free transmission of information.

Over the years, Christine and I have become co-mentors and friends. We share the same excitement and wonder at how easy it is to do yet so few people are willing to take the time to learn the tricks of the trade. It is now Christine's turn to share what she has learned through the years. She has a somewhat different take on the travel game, different from my own, but what I admire about her is that she knows how to get the most from her travel dollar and utilizes the limited time she has on weekends to get out there and see the world. Christine knows her stuff and conveys it in a humorous and practical manner.

Personally I wouldn't do all that traveling just on the weekend but we are all different. That is the beauty of this group; we all look at the travel experience differently but we all carry this same message to you the "newbie" or "rookie" whichever term you prefer:

You can do this. You can see the world at prices you can afford.

Rick, the Frugal Travel Guy

www.frugaltravelguy.com

Introduction

By Christine

How it started -- the world in a weekend thing, that is.

I posed the question to several people when I found a $300 airfare to Paris: "Want to go to Paris this weekend?" My friend replied, "Only the weekend? No, I want to go when I can do it right. I'd rather spend that money on a nice suit for work." Then there was my sister: "You mean take only Friday off and go all the way to Paris?" I asked another friend: "Well, let me think about it and get back to you."

I went off to Paris for the weekend...alone.

I gave up my seat on the first flight of my journey since it was oversold and received a $400 voucher good for future travel, a fair sacrifice that only set my journey back a few hours. This amount was more than I paid for the original ticket. Once in Paris, I stayed in a little boutique hotel for $60 a night, which included breakfast. This was before I had any knowledge of what hotel points were. For dinner I ate three dollar Brie, tomato, and cucumber baguettes on the street (they're still my favorite). I saw the Eiffel tower for the first time! It was the greatest weekend and I spent very little. I was hooked and I wanted to do it again!

I started seeking out cheap fares wherever I could find them. I didn't care if they were to Timbuktu. All the better, I thought. Who do I know who's been to Timbuktu?

I didn't know it then but I had wanderlust. I learned later that you either have it or you don't. And once it's activated, nothing can hold you back. You have to go and discover the world.

You have to.

When I look back at my childhood, I realize I had it even then. Wanderlust, I mean. I grew up in the woods of Northern Michigan and the woods were where I wandered at that point in my life. At age eight my mother took me to a book sale at the library where I acquired a world atlas from the 1920s. I still have it. I circled the places in the world I would go. They were flat, black and white faded pages, for gosh sakes -- why would I want to go there? Because I had wanderlust!

At age twelve (in the days before strict child labor laws), I took a job in a bakery and saved up enough money by age fifteen to buy a moped that got me to work, but more importantly it allowed me to go further.

There was a gap in my wandering years after I became a single parent, but I never had travel boundaries and soon my son and I, with very little money, were driving off to Kentucky to fish, or to Vermont to ski for one day because

I found a half price coupon. I was always looking to see how far we could go for very little money.

Fast-forward to my corporate working years where I had a lot of paid vacation time and didn't know what to do with it. I read a book called *Smart Vacations*. It was a book about spending your vacation time productively. I found a couple trips I really liked, including one where I would stay in an apartment in Vienna and take German language lessons during the day. Hey, my mom's family was German – I could do that. So I did! The following year I went to Thailand and rode elephants and visited the hill tribes. Then I went to Nepal and hiked in the Himalayas and, subsequently, went off to Africa and climbed Mt. Kilimanjaro.

The corporate years ended and I became self-employed with no paid vacation and a business that does not allow me to be gone for any length of time without things deteriorating significantly. But I still had wanderlust, and now, a budget.

In 2001, I found a cheap weekend fare to Mexico City and met a guy from Grand Rapids, Michigan, who told me about a new travel site online: www.flyertalk.com. I signed up and have been a fan ever since. I've learned about how to find cheap fares, accumulate miles and points, and attain status with the airlines. This knowledge has allowed me to travel cheaply (even free), in style, and use the limited amount of time I have on the weekends to experience the world in way I never would have imagined.

Why would *you* want to see the world in a weekend? Taking long plane trips to earn frequent flyer miles and see a foreign city for a day is not everyone's cup of tea. However, if you have a strong desire to travel, a tight budget, and limited time to do it, you may be open to some ideas to help you explore the world that up until now, you never thought you would see or experience.

This is the ultimate result of seeing the world in a weekend but the tips you will learn in this book can help with something as simple as an annual vacation. I know friends, family and co-workers who learned enough to plan a luxury trip for very little, even free. One friend takes his entire family of five to Hawaii for ten days and all of their airfare, hotel, and most of their food expenses are free! You could do that too.

My purpose in writing this book is not to encourage you to see the world in a weekend, it is to inspire you to travel in a different way, a no-barriers, don't need to spend thousands of dollars, way. Maybe when you read this you will at least consider that there are whole new possibilities out there and use this knowledge to create your own special travel experience.

Now I'd like to share some of that knowledge, and some of my experiences, with you.

How to see the World in a Weekend - Part 1

Planning that spring break to Daytona Beach, once again? Spending a couple thousand bucks and driving home with burnt skin and a hangover? Those days should be behind you, they're well....so last decade. Try this on for size: you have a few hundred dollars and want to get out of town and try something new and exciting. I'm talking exciting: Latin America, Europe, Central America or even Asia. Think it can't happen? You are about to learn that this is exactly what can happen when you are exposed to traveling in a whole different way and then act on what you learn. You may embrace it, reject it, or not "get" it at all but one thing for sure, you'll consider the possibility; some of you may even become addicted and never travel any other way.

Going where everyone else goes at the same time everyone else wants to go there is expensive; it's the law of supply and demand. In addition, it is generally neither a good value for your travel dollar nor a particularly unique experience. You don't have to do that anymore. In the past you would have said, "I have to go when the kids are out of school" or "I have to go between Christmas and New Years because that's when my place of employment is closed". And there are a thousand more reasons to keep traveling the way you've been traveling: the end result being that you will do what you have done before, experience the same experiences, and see what you have already seen, and you will spend more money making it all happen. It's time to snap out of it! If you're willing to think differently about your travels, your experiences will change and they will change for the better.

The adventure truly begins when you throw away the destination; chuck it, forget it, abandon it! You know *when* you're going; you just don't know *where* you're going. This one critical step, in itself, will change the way you travel. For instance, you may have five allotted travel days, however because you have not selected a destination, you have opened up the possibility of going anywhere in the world, yes, anywhere. Let's hope you've gotten your passport by now so you can play on other playgrounds, not just the United States.

Now comes the hard part; how do you determine where you're going? Let's go back to our reasons for considering this seemingly absurd idea: to travel more cost effectively, to experience new and exciting places, or just to become a more interesting person. You will go places few of your friends have gone and you will have unique experiences to share; this alone makes you interesting. An added benefit is what happens to you while you are in transit to these new and different places, transit stories can turn out to be more interesting than those at the destination. The process of finding the best destination to fit your budget and one that you would be willing to explore begins with some research. There are several web sites that will assist us in determining where to go, techniques that will help you get the most travel for the least amount of money and out-of-the-box, over-the-top, insane ways to manipulate existing promotions for free or nearly free hotels, rental cars, and flights. If it sounds like I'm promising you the world, well in a way, I am. But I won't ask you to do anything I wouldn't do myself. .

How to see the World in a Weekend – Part Two

Previously I introduced the concept of traveling without a pre-determined destination in mind in order to travel more cost-effectively, explore new and exciting places and perhaps gain the added benefit of making ourselves a bit more interesting. If you were even mildly intrigued by the idea, by now you're hungry for more information. Since I've got your attention, it's time to deliver.

I proposed that instead of traveling to the same destination everyone else wants to visit when they want to go there, spending top dollar, and doing the same thing every year, why not travel when you choose, find a destination that is "on sale", and set no boundaries as to where that final destination might be. However, right now you may be asking yourself: "How do I find these deals?" It's not an exact science, it's a treasure hunt and you know what you can find on a treasure hunt so I'll get you started in the right direction.

There are web sites that allow you to plug in your preferred departure airport and search for cities throughout the world that happen to have the lowest fares. Your first step in determining where you will go on your trip is to visit one of these sites. One of my favorites is www.farecompare.com. The site offers a tool called "Getaway Deals Map" which will help you start your treasure hunt. Click on this option; plug in the three letter code for your home airport, and a world map populated with the best fare deals will pop up. Another web site to use is www.kayak.com/buzz; also with a destination map that offers deals from any airport you plug in. When you're a bit more savvy, you can move on to matrix.itasoftware.com; a great site requiring some homework, learning how to utilize it. Go to one of these sites and type in your desired departure airport. Wow, look at all the possibilities! Sometimes it can be cheaper to go to Europe than to go to Florida; so why not go to Europe?! You could be sleeping in your bed tonight and wake up in your bedroom or you could be sleeping on a plane and wake up in Paris! You can even set up alerts that will come to you in the form of an email when airfare deals develop from your home airport. Who knows where you'll be going next!

I'll warn you that not every search ends successfully. Airfares change daily, even hourly and you may need to do several searches on different days before scoring the fare that fits your schedule and budget. You can also try nearby airports for your departure as this may open up a whole new set of destination cities from which to choose. Once you've found a deal you like, Farecompare.com will direct you to the airline's web site so you can book directly.

Now if you compare this out-of-the-box traveling to a video game, you've barely made it to level one. You've decided to fly somewhere but you won't know where until you find that little gem of an airfare that sets your heart pumping. You'll score and it will feel good. It will feel so good; you'll want to do it again. Let's just take a deep breath and make sure you're maximizing this new found travel freedom. First, you'll want to make sure you've signed up for the airline frequent flier program so you can start earning miles. Earning miles can get you to the next level: STATUS. Now you're cooking; you'll be earning perks such as upgrades, free tickets, no luggage fees, and early boarding. Traveling to exciting places is great but you want to make sure you're earning miles and perks that can get you even more discounted or even free trips in the future.

OK, you've now booked your bargain airfare but we still need to find a great deal on a hotel room. Hey, what do you say we kick it up a notch and try to get a FREE hotel room? Stay tuned for *How to see the World in a Weekend, Part Three* where we'll continue our journey towards experiencing travel the way it should be.

How to see the World in a Weekend – Part Three

We continue on our World in a Weekend journey with the premise that having a pre-determined destination when you travel is detrimental to the pocketbook and taking that annual two week vacation to the same beachfront condo may get in the way of you seeing the rest of the world. Oh, and by the way, it doesn't make you much more interesting that you were last year. If you can consider visiting a country you have never been to at a cheap price, you could visit several countries a year and not spend as much as you do on a two-week vacation to Boca Del Vista. Let me ask you a tough question: "if you could go to Australia for cheap (or free) but you only had a few days to do it….would you go?" By now, maybe you're warming up to the idea that you have the option to reevaluate how and where you travel.

Now let's recap where we've been: we've gone to www.farecompare.com, typed in our home airport, searched the world for the cheapest ticket we could find outside of the United States and scored a deal on airfare to Istanbul (for example). I use this example because I recently booked such a deal to Istanbul for Thanksgiving. Now, finding a cheap hotel is not a difficult task but with some preplanning you can stay in more upscale digs just as cheaply. In addition, you can take advantage of some sweet perks and even earn free rooms. The first step in getting these great hotel deals is to sign up for a few hotel loyalty programs. Some of the more popular ones are Hilton (www.hiltonhonors.com), Starwood Preferred Guest (www.spg.com), Intercontinental/Holiday Inn (www.priorityclub.com), Marriott (www.marriottrewards.com) and Hyatt Gold Passport (www.hyatt.com). Once you've signed up, the emails will start flowing into your inbox and the deals will be there for the taking. Your benefits also begin immediately as you gain such perks as late checkouts, free newspapers, free local phone calls, free internet access, and even room upgrades. My rule is that I never stay at a hotel or motel chain without joining their frequent stay program, never. I do not want to miss out on future offers that may bring me perks and/or free rooms. With my membership in these frequent stay programs I'm privy to the real deals like a recent promotion where you stay 2 nights and get a certificate for a third night free. Here's the beauty of such a promotion: you stay twice in one of their cheapest hotels (in this case it was $59/night), earn your free certificate and use it for a room at one of their top notch resorts in Hawaii for example, which costs over $400 a night. FREE. I know because I've done it and so have many of my friends. I actually used free night certificates for high-end hotel rooms in Copenhagen, Toronto, Rome, Quito, Helsinki, and Hawaii, all within a year.

We've booked our cheap air ticket and our hotel and now we're off to see the world in a weekend. I use the term *weekend* loosely as it can certainly mean taking a long weekend or an extended holiday weekend which I frequently have to do because I still have a real job. But I do challenge you to stretch yourself and plan your next trip without a pre-determined destination and see what might present itself; you may just end up in Istanbul for Thanksgiving.

Well, we've just scratched the surface in our quest for cheap travel but hopefully by now you're starting to think you actually can see the world in a weekend.

A Passport: Your Ticket To The Rest of the World

I once read a quote that said, "The only two things you need in life are a corkscrew and a passport." Believe it or not, there are people out there who don't drink wine and even more who don't own a passport.

I'm determined to convince the entire population of the United States to get one. A passport, that is. I'll work on recruiting more wine drinkers later.

How did you get to this point in your life without owning a passport? According to the Yale Center of the Study of Globalization, only 21 percent of Americans own a passport. The study also found that Americans travel less than their worldly counterparts. Why own a passport when you never leave the United States?

The baby boomer generation (born 1946-1964) may be just the group up to the job of changing those dynamics. This large group with their overall zest to travel and enjoy life will likely have an impact on the percentages of Americans who have a passport. If you have a passport, you already know why you should have one. If you don't have a passport, there are more reasons than ever for you to consider getting one. Picture these scenarios: Your best friend wins a trip to Paris and wants you to go. You can't. The fish are biting in Canada. You can't go. Your son decides at the last minute to get married in Acapulco. You're going to miss it. And so on.

What else can you do with a passport?

- Volunteer
- Discover new cultures
- Learn a new language
- Make that pilgrimage
- Find your ancestors
- See a new ocean
- Discover architecture older than anything you'll ever see in the U.S.
- Find out how the rest of the world lives
- Buy a treasure you can't find at home
- Eat new foods
- Experience new music
- See rare animals and plants in their natural environment
- See very large mountains
- Learn new history
- Walk in ancient gardens
- Visit Roman ruins

- Find out how perfume is made

- Participate in a harvest

- Cruise on exotic rivers

- Visit the site of a famous battle

- Walk on distant shores

- Enjoy a festival

Perhaps you'd like to see all of the New Seven Wonders of the World.* (Do you even know where, or what, they are? I'll tell you in a moment.)

OK, now I have to warn you: If you put "get a passport" on your to-do list, your chances of getting it done are slim. Getting a passport is a process and you will need to finish each step to get it done right.

Step 1: Get your passport photo. You can do this at most drug stores these days. How about this: Next time you're waiting to get your prescription filled, walk over and get your passport photos taken. *Bam!* Two birds with one stone.

Step 2: Find your original birth certificate. If you don't have one, order it from the courthouse in the county where you were born.

Step 3: Pick up a passport application. You can do this at the post office, your county seat, or even where you had your passport photo taken. Our local post office holds passport events where they will walk you through the whole process from photo to submitting the application. Maybe your local post office does the same. Or you can go directly to the State Department's web site, http://travel.state.gov/passport/passport_1738.html, and print out the needed forms. That site also does a great job of walking you through the necessary steps.

Yes, I've heard all the excuses for not getting a passport, including, "There are so many places I still have to see in the United States," and "I don't want the government to track where I go," and "I will never need it," and even "I can't afford to go anywhere." All valid in your own mind, but listen up: Times have changed. You won't be able to go on a simple fishing trip to Canada without a passport. Passport = Freedom. Along with your birth certificate, driver's license, and Social Security card, it is one of the most important documents you will ever own and your ticket to the rest of the world.

If you still aren't convinced that you need a passport, here's a little book I recommend: *Don't let the world pass you by! 52 reasons to get a passport*, published by Lonely Planet.

*By the way -- The New Seven Wonders of the World, according to the 2007 Swiss-based New7Wonders

Foundation, are: The Great Wall of China, The Coliseum in Rome, The Taj Mahal in India, The Christ Redeemer Statue in Brazil, Petra in Jordan, Machu Picchu in Peru, and Chichen Itza in Mexico, and an honorary 8th place going to the Pyramids of Giza in Egypt.

How to become a Millionaire….A Frequent Flyer Millionaire that is.

A million dollars doesn't buy as much as it used to and neither does a million frequent flyer miles. This doesn't mean you shouldn't strive to earn a million dollars or not try to build a bank of a million frequent flyer miles; just know that inflation and devaluation eat away at both nest eggs.

I have such a nest egg, a million frequent flyer miles and people ask me all the time how I accumulate so many. Truth is I know a lot of people with many more miles and a lot more savvy than I and due to the fact that you can earn these miles in so many ways, Frequent Flyer Millionaires are being created out there every day. There is no reason you can't be one too however so let's explore the ways to earn these miles and then put a plan together to become a Frequent Flyer Millionaire. I'll start with the basics then add my own **XM (extra miles) option** to step it up a notch and accelerate your earnings. I always do the XM Option but earning miles is a personal thing and as a newbie you will have to learn what you are willing and not willing to do to accumulate miles. For a start, here are the basic ways to accumulate frequent flyer miles:

1. Flying on mile-earning flights

2. Earning status and receive bonus miles

3. Open a credit card or bank account that offers a sign–up bonus

4. Buy things via the airlines shopping site

5. Sign up for bonuses/promotions

6. Buy miles or Transfer miles

7. Charge items on your airline credit card

8. Convert points to miles

I estimate that I've earned over five million miles doing all of the above of which about 1.8 million were actually flown miles. Let's explore what it takes to be a Frequent Flyer Millionaire.

Flying on mile-earning flights: This is a no-brainer: buy a mileage-earning ticket and fly it. You will earn the miles you flew. You can earn more flown miles if you buy a ticket at a fare that is in a higher premium class, usually 50% more miles. The airlines web site is the best resource for determining how many miles you will earn; go to their frequent flyer program and look for "earn miles".

My XM Option: Add a lot of extra segments to your flight when you have a flexible schedule and watch the miles add up.

Earn status and receive bonus miles: If you fly enough miles to earn status with the airline, typically starting at

25,000 flown miles, you can earn bonus miles in addition to flight miles. Usually only flown miles count towards elite status (with the exception of a few credit card offerings and flyer program rules) and bonus miles do not but all are usually spendable miles.

My XM Option: Some carriers boost your minimum miles per segment flown to 500 miles when you reach elite status. For example, the flight may be only 217 flown miles but you receive the minimum 500 because you achieved their elite status level.

Open a credit card or bank account that offers a sign up bonus: Frequent flyer millionaires probably got most of their accumulated miles from this option.

My XM Option: Research the best options available. The Frugal Travel Guy blog is the best site I know of if you're looking for information on credit card and bank account bonuses, and I visit this site nearly every day. Frequentflyer.com also has a nice breakdown of options.

Buy things on the airline shopping site: Most items or services you would normally purchase you can buy via the shopping area of the airlines own web site; so why not earn miles for these purchases?! Once again, go to "earn miles" and you'll see a shopping option.

My XM Option: Some retailers offer more miles per dollar spent than others. Frequent Flyer Millionaires never buy anything without earning miles or points whether it's a simple coffee at McDonalds or a $5000 flat screen TV.

Sign up for bonuses/promotions: Airlines offer bonuses for flying between certain city pairs, promotions where you receive double flown miles, and other offers where you can earn additional miles. Once again, the airlines web site is a good source for finding these offers but once you've signed up for their frequent flyer program, you will receive some of these offers in your email.

My XM Option: Seek out these promotions on sites like www.flyertalk.com or by just typing in a request such as *American Airlines miles promotion* into your search engine. Don't avoid a particular promotion because you don't think you'll use it, sign up for them all and sometimes you'll get the miles anyway.

Buy miles or Transfer Miles: Airlines offer you the option to purchase miles or transfer them from another account. This option for accumulating miles is an expensive one and not recommended unless you need a small amount of miles to reach enough for a ticket.

My XM Option: On occasion, airlines offer bonus options for buying and/or transferring miles between accounts. In some cases these bonuses can reach 100 percent. So if you were to purchase/transfer 10,000 miles, the airline would give you 10,000 miles. In this case it's a much better deal and worth considering.

Charge items on your airline credit card: Most people know this method and try to build a big bank of miles for a family vacation this way. You can definitely earn miles this way, but it can be a slow process.

My XM Option: Do your research and find out if the card gives double, triple, or even greater bonuses when you use it for particular items, then designate that card for those purchases. For example, if your Delta card gives you double miles for Delta purchases that is the card you would use for those purchases. If your Chase Visa card offers three miles for every dollar you spend on groceries, use that card for groceries.

Convert points to miles: Some credit card programs offer "points" versus miles. These points can be cashed in for travel or in some cases, converted to miles. You should evaluate which option equates to a better value.

My XM Option: Check the conversion rules to see if there is a fixed option. For example, for 20,000 points you may be able to get a domestic airline ticket that is valued up to

$250, whereas by using points to purchase travel, the value may be only $200.

Another way to become a Frequent Flier Millionaire is to not spend your frequent flier miles – to save and accumulate them first. I am guilty of this. I hate flying without earning miles so I have a hard time spending my miles on flights for myself. I use my miles so that friends and family can tag along and to position myself for cheap fare deals I may have booked from an airport other than my home airport. However, miles continue to devalue as their availability increases, so I highly recommend spending them while they're worth as much as they ever will be. And when you do hit a million, take a snapshot of your statement then go on an airline ticket spending spree and travel the world for free!

The Art of the "Bump"

If you do your homework, plan some extra time in your travel schedule, and take initiative at the departure gate, you may be able to earn some extra travel dollars.

I am asked quite frequently how I can afford to travel to so many places. The explanation is multi-faceted but most of my travel dollars have come from denied boarding vouchers. The availability of these sacred vouchers has declined somewhat but they're still out there for the taking if you plan ahead and be proactive in your approach.

When airlines sell tickets for a particular flight, they sometimes oversell a flight based on the assumption that some passengers will not show. It is not an illegal practice and most of the time it works out just fine. In some cases however, the flight ends up oversold and there are more confirmed passengers than seats. In these cases, the airline will ask for volunteers to give up their seats and in return they will issue a voucher for future air travel, meal tickets and hotel accommodations if appropriate. This practice is known in the travel hacker world as a "bump". These vouchers can range from $200 to whatever the airline determines is a fair price to pay to open up the necessary seats. I recently scored a $500 voucher and a $10 meal coupon for a flight from San Juan, Puerto Rico to Miami when I gave up my seat. Most of the time however, I receive the standard $400 and once I took a $250 voucher in return for taking a flight that left two hours later. International flights bring higher voucher denominations due to the length of the flight and amount of time until the next departure.

How can you accumulate your own travel kitty from collecting denied boarding vouchers? First, you have to do your homework as to which flights you'll select, plan extra time for your journey, and then be proactive in your approach once you get to your departure gate.

Do your homework:

It would make sense that if you want to be on an oversold flight that you book a flight where most of the seats are already taken. You would probably think accordingly that seats sell out because there is high demand and this can drive the price up so purchasing a flight with few (or no) seats available may be costly. Most of the time you would be correct, in some cases however I have purchased the last seat for no more that I would have paid normally. Other times, when I purchase the ticket, there are NO seats available; a good sign but it doesn't mean everyone is going to show up or that all available seats have been assigned. It just means I have a better chance of the flight being oversold.

An example: Let's say you're going to Orlando for spring break; chances are you'll be paying a premium for your tickets anyway. Selecting the flight that is the fullest, planning your schedule so you have time to take advantage of a bump possibility, and asking the gate agent if they need volunteers may result in you earning a nice voucher to pay for your next trip. Keep in mind that seat maps don't always show all of the available seats due to premium seats being held or some exit/bulkhead row seats being blocked for later assignment.

Flexible Schedule

In order to take advantage of the bump possibility, you need to plan extra time in your travel day(s). While this isn't always possible, even a few hours can make the difference. If you were planning on leaving in the afternoon, reconsider and select a morning flight to increase your chances of being able to accept a bump should one be offered.

Be Proactive

It doesn't hurt to go up and ask if the flight is oversold and if they need volunteers.

Finally, keep in mind that new legislation increasing the amount airlines must compensate passengers who are involuntarily denied boarding has somewhat diminished the availability of flights being oversold. They still happen daily however so why not prepare yourself and build your own little travel fund.

Surviving the Long Plane Ride

I get asked frequently how I can go half way around the world in a weekend without major jet lag. When it comes to long plane rides, we all cope in our own way but how well we cope may begin with planning. Here are some tips I have gathered from my traveling friends as well as techniques I use myself to survive, even thrive during those long hours on a plane:

Boredom

What can you do to keep from being bored on a long flight? There are always the crossword puzzle doers, the video game players and the DVD watchers but aside from the obvious, how can you make a long flight interesting?

First, try making your dining experience on the plane an affair to remember: Bring a selection of the best foods and create a picnic. Bring a little checkered tablecloth (a large table napkin, plastic tablecloth cut smaller or any piece of fabric will work), top quality plastic wine glasses, olives, cheese, crackers, salami, artichokes, humus, a baguette, and any other foods that would serve to generate envy from fellow passengers (and flight attendants) when you start setting up your dining experience. Believe me, this makes you feel special and everyone around you wishes they had done it too. They're sitting in their cramped seats waiting for airline food and you're dining in style. You can also use the wine glasses and tablecloth later during your trip for a "bed picnic" in your hotel room.

I bring along a stack of magazines that I have not had a chance to read. I tear out any interesting items I want to follow up on and then leave the magazine in the seat pocket. As the trip goes on, my bag gets lighter and lighter. Flight attendants also appreciate these so be sure to offer the magazines to them when they pass through the aisle.

Visit the used book store before you leave on your trip. I find Goodwill a great place to pick up a few used books for fifty cents or a dollar and I always have something in my bag to read. If you finish the book while on your trip you can leave it along the way for another traveler to enjoy.

Write. Bring a blank journal and write about your trip. Doesn't matter if you're not a writer, you'll still enjoy looking back and reading about the experience; it is surprising how much you forget over time.

Load your pictures to your laptop and sort them. This is something my friend is always doing; she is so smart. I never take the time to organize my pictures but sitting on a plane would be the perfect time to do so.

Getting some Sleep

I have traveled so much that I can now sleep on a plane, no problem. It's just like a ride on Sunday afternoon in the family car; as soon as the plane starts moving, I'm out. It wasn't always that way, I was wide awake for hours but I have become accustomed to the ritual and as soon as I get on the plane I start arranging my little crib for a nice nap. In the winter I bring my fluffy down jacket and a satin pillow case (black works best) and I stuff the jacket into the pillow case and enjoy a nice comfy base to sleep on. And because the pillow case is satin, there are no sleep lines on your face when you wake up.

My friend takes a natural herb supplement that helps her sleep and she swears by it. I have known travelers who have taken prescription sleeping aids but with various results, mostly difficulty waking up fully at the end of a flight as the flight duration may be less than the required eight hours most medications require. They can still offer an effective way of getting a few hours of necessary rest if you plan accordingly.

Hygiene and Comfort

I try to bring a pair of lightweight slippers for walking on the plane and entering the bathroom; your feet are protected but comfortable. The slippers you get in hotel rooms work well and you can dispose of them after your plane ride. A pack of wet wipes can offer refreshment and keep your hands clean throughout the flight; my favorite being baby wipes as they smell so good and don't dry out your skin with too much alcohol.

I recently discovered saline nasal sprays that keep the nasal passage moisturized thus making it easier to breathe and reduce the chance of getting congested. I have heard this is a product that airline pilots also use; there are several available for purchase over the counter. After visiting my optometrist for eye allergies, he recommended GenTeal Gel, a clear lubricant gel that liquefies in the eye and keeps your eyes moisturized; great product for use during flight. He suggested avoiding products that reduce redness due to their drying effect.

And for that last portion of the flight just before landing, I bring along some teeth-whitening strips as a back-up to use just in case. They don't take the place of brushing your teeth at the end of a long flight but sometimes you're not able to so they help by killing some germs and brightening your smile a bit. Now you're ready for immigration!

With a little preparation, your plane flight will pass quickly and you will feel like you used the time productively or at least your time onboard didn't suck.

Change your Mindset and Travel the World for Free

How do you see the World in a Weekend for free or nearly free? It starts by living your life differently. You view everyday transactions as opportunities to earn points/miles that earn you free travel. You find ways to sneak out of work early to leave for a weekend in Europe. Or if you're retired, you tell your grown children that you're cleaning the garage this weekend when you're really off to a free weekend in Mexico. Yes, sometimes there is deceit involved but seldom more than little white travel lies. You see if you don't hide some of your travel, your friends, family, and co-workers will think that you actually pay for your trips and therefore wrongly conclude you are rich. This phenomenon can lead to resentment and requests for loans so trust me, don't brag about *all* of your new found travel freedom.

When you've obsessed with traveling the world for free or nearly free, you seek opportunities for points and miles. Here's an example: I'm in the McDonalds drive-thru and I see a sign: It seems like a simple incentive; purchase a $10 McDonald's gift card and get a free coffee. I start to think, "If I buy 10 cards for $100, I will get 10 free cups of coffee for a total value of $17.00 or 17% return on my money. Hmmm, I will certainly use the gift cards in the future or give them as gifts to my nieces and nephews. I will charge them with my Chase Freedom card and get 500 points plus 10 points for the transaction. Good deal? The jury is out but it's more about the process of looking at your purchases differently on a consistent basis. Ask yourself, "How will this transaction benefit me the most in my quest for free travel and give me good value for my money?"

I've set some new simple personal ground rules for earning points/miles:

50,000 miles/points is my benchmark for opening a new credit card. Sometimes there are deals with fewer incentives that offer other benefits but 50,000 is my benchmark to take that minor credit hit.

Never pay cash for any purchase when I can use miles or point-earning credit cards. Yes, even my $1.70 cup of coffee earns me bonus points for the transaction. (Yes, I even charge my auto and home insurance.)

Never book a long haul round-trip mileage award ticket without adding on an extra (shorter) free segment. Yes, the airlines will let you do this.

Always offer to pay for the meal when you're in a group, collect cash from everyone for their share then put the total on your points/miles earning credit card. Determine which cards have bonus miles for dining purchases and be sure to use those cards.

Look for deals on a daily basis to earn bonus miles for small purchases I would be making any way.

Never stay at a hotel/motel or rent a car without earning or spending points.

Sign up for as many airline, hotel, and rental car promotions as humanly possible to multiply my earning power opportunities.

Refer friends for deals/cards/promotions that offer referral bonuses.

If you are a person who does mostly cash transactions, changing your mindset must seem daunting and this game may not be for you. But if you're willing to think about the extra value you can achieve by rethinking your daily routine and you have the discipline, you can reap travel rewards you never thought possible.

Security in the Fast Lane

There I was in the arrival hall of the international terminal; there must have been three hundred people in line waiting to pass through immigration. I had a little over an hour to connect to the last flight of the day to my destination.....home. There was no way I was going to make the connecting flight, having to spend the night in Chicago and subsequently miss nearly an entire day of work. It was at that moment that I decided I needed to apply for Global Entry, the new expediting service that allows you to scan your passport into a kiosk and zip through immigration.

I have avoided applying for this service because in order to be approved, you must have an interview with Homeland Security and answer a lot of questions about your travels. I imagined that the interview would go like this: "No I don't travel for work, sir. Yes, I do take a lot of weekend trips to other parts of the world. No, I am not rich. Well, you see I try to get the cheapest flight I can and travel as far as I can to get the frequent flier miles and hopefully spend a day in a foreign city. Yes, I know that this is not normal. No, I don't remember where I went in February of 2010, maybe Paris, perhaps Istanbul, possibly Berlin? Yes you're right; it was Athens, now I remember. You see I just got a new passport because the other one was full so I don't remember all the countries in the order of when I was there."

Regardless of my fears of such an interview, I made the decision to apply online and set the process in motion. It cost $100 to apply but this fee included acceptance into the Trusted Traveler Program and eligibility for Pre-screen, a new service offered by the airlines where you don't have to remove your shoes, your liquids, or your laptop. I was approved within days and along with the approval confirmation email came the invitation to set up the dreaded interview. I made my appointment online for the Chicago airport facility and showed up on time, ready for the interrogation. I had memorized everywhere I had been this year and created helpful mnemonics (thank you Ms. Grigsby, fifth grade teacher) to assist me. I was ready.

Then, the interview went something like this: "What type of work do you do? Do you travel for work? How did you hear about the program? Have you ever been convicted of a crime?" There were a few more questions regarding birthplace, name, and other questions that were basically factual of which I knew all of the answers, but then I was done! The rest was instructional on how to use the program. The whole session took about 17 minutes. Hey, wait a minute! Didn't they care that I went half way around the world in a weekend? Didn't they want to know why I went to Kazakhstan for only a day? Didn't they want to hear about my travels and how I find all of these deals? Didn't they want to see my business card that says I am a travel writer? I guess I should be happy it went so smoothly and now I can make that one hour connection in

Chicago to catch my flight home; for that I am eternally grateful.

If you want to apply for Global Entry (and I highly recommend it), go to www.globalentry.com

Drag Queens & Dervishes

Whether it's a great band serving up dance tunes, a ragingly funny standup comic or a jazz session creating a background for engaging conversation, we all like to be entertained. While I don't necessarily seek out entertainment when I travel, inevitably an invitation to join in is extended to me. Some entertainment decisions turn out to be more memorable than others.

It started with SARS (severe acute respiratory syndrome). The fear of infection kept people off planes to Asia and the resulting empty planes created a window of cheap ($350-$500) round-trip airfares to places like Hong Kong, mainland China and Singapore. It was on one of these excursions where I discovered Singapore's true entertainment delight: the trans-gender drag queen cabaret nightclub. While I had attended a similar show in Acapulco, this was nothing like the raucous display in Singapore. A mix of off color jaw dropping comedic talent, frequently changing vibrant costumes and great dance moves, I was thrilled and amazed at Singapore's Boom Boom Room production. During intermission I even enjoyed dancing to current tunes along with the performers and audience. It was such an unlikely venue for this extravaganza but an experience I found unforgettable in a good way; trust me on this.

Then there was the night I ate raisin covered lamb on the floor of a Sultan's Tent. The belly dancers were mesmerizing, throwing their hips in instinctive directions and keeping in perfect time with the enchanting music. Perhaps it was a concerted attempt to charm a snake from the clay pot sitting next to me. The swirling dancers with their jingling brass adornments were just hints that I was not in a familiar country but perhaps some far off desert land with my camel waiting outside the tent. Who would have thought I was in Toronto! The Sultan's Tent restaurant has been a favorite of mine for many years but is now a bit more modern; no sitting amongst pillows on the floor and eating off brass trays. The wonderful Moroccan food with a French twist, authentic entertainment that complements the decor, and the flowing fabric and throw pillows to emulate your own private sultan's tent makes it a must-visit. www.TheSultansTent.com

While I'm willing to pay for good entertainment, nothing beats the discovery of a free performance when you least expect it. It happened in Chang Mai, Thailand, at the night market. A full day of adventure, riding elephants in the jungles of northern Thailand, and I was ready to put my feet up with a tall glass of salted guava juice (a local favorite). The stage lights up, the music begins, and in front of my eyes are some of the most beautiful women I have ever seen. Their costumes were of fine brightly colored silk complementing headdresses of gold and their dance moves were of precision and beauty. A traditional Thai dance is one lovely feast for the senses. The eerie music of the flutes and other ancient Asian instruments transports you to a special place. And all this happened in the flurry of night market shopping... awesome.

A surreal evening surrounded by Whirling Dervishes stays at the top of my most memorable entertainment list. Although not originally intended for entertainment, the meditative dance performed to ancient hypnotic music is now shared with interested tourists. Sitting in a dark train station in the heart of Istanbul, Turkey, we watch the performers in their wide flowing skirts and tall smooth cone-like hats spinning and spinning for what seems like eternity. The striking attire represents the letting go of the ego, a necessary element to entering their trance. This Sufi ritual is performed in an effort to achieve religious ecstasy by the dancing Dervishes but is truly a unique experience for the spectators as well and one not soon forgotten.

As I reflect, I realize that many of my favorite entertainment experiences have come about as the result of accepting an invitation, surely a clear message to accept future invitations. After all, it's certainly an entertaining world out there.

Bed Picnics – Rated G

The nightly restaurant ritual while we're traveling can become expensive, result in long waits due to summer crowds, and eventually verge on restaurant overload. You may just prefer a simple meal enjoyed quietly with that special someone, dining in with the family, or treating yourself to a solo supper. Whether you're held up in a condo, hotel room, or you're planning an evening at home, a "bed picnic" may be just the alternative to this nightly dining-out repetition.

It all begins when you make the decision to have your own bed picnic; yes, the fact that I have termed it a "bed picnic" indicates it will indeed take place on a bed. Select one evening of your trip (or your normal working week for that matter) and designate it as bed picnic night. You then set out for a day of exploring with a secondary objective of foraging for food items for your twilight picnic. Each city or region is its own bed picnic super market so spend your day searching and discovering the bountiful selection of edible delights you'll look forward to indulging in this evening. You'll find an endless array of choices: perhaps a bottle (or two) of wine from a local vineyard, locally produced cheeses, freshly grown fruits and vegetables from roadside markets, specialty meats and smoked fish, a fresh-baked loaf of artisan bread from a brick oven, pastries from a local bakery, and specialty olive oil, vinegars, and olives, just to name some of my favorites. You'll surely find your own edible treasures.

Now it's evening and time to reap the rewards of your food-foraging activities. Prepare the bed with a "tablecloth" of paper bags or purchase one of those inexpensive plastic red and white checkered cloths you're sure to come across in your daily travels. It will wash off nicely and you can use it again and again; this isn't your last bed picnic, you know! No rules here except that you enjoy the spread you've put together. There's a certain satisfaction gained from the fact that you gathered the food during your travels and anticipated the upcoming picnic you'd be sharing with others. No lines, no expensive restaurant check, just pure fresh local food you and your family personally selected. Best of all, your bed picnic is one-of-a-kind; there will never be another one exactly like this one because of how it was created. You can visit another city and create another bed picnic but it will be totally different, equally as wonderful perhaps, but totally different dependent on the season and local specialties available.

So go out, forage and enjoy the best the area you're visiting has to offer. Oh yes, and tomorrow night I know this little French restaurant you might be interested in.

Kissing the American Toilet

I would venture to say that most of us take our American toilet for granted. We can thank the English for this sacred invention; initially with a crude model back in the late 1500's and the more modern flushable version a couple hundred years later. I just want to thank the English publicly for this indispensable invention.

You see most people in the world lack the convenience of a modern toilet like ours. I remember the day, the exact day that I first became aware of this fact and personally experienced this cold reality. I was traveling in Africa in the back of a pickup truck when nature yelled at me, "you need a bathroom FAST!" The truck pulled over and I was immediately escorted to a strange wooden "room" in the back of a very modest restaurant we might in America refer to as a roadside shack. I'm sure the cuisine was exceptional as the "bathroom" was certainly a room with a view, a 4 ft x 4 ft stall with a hole in the back wall right at eye level where you could see the mountains or conveniently enough, the mountains could see you. The jagged hole in the wood was strange enough but as I instantly scanned the micro stall, I could find no suitable, let me rephrase that, no freaking place to sit whatsoever. No time to ponder the circumstances however, I needed to grasp the situation quickly and get down to business. Now, I'm a fairly limber person but the gyrations needed to navigate this toilet were more than demanding.

There were two porcelain foot markers which I brilliantly determined were where my feet should be placed; although inconveniently they were not marked as to which foot should be placed where. Continuing to be puzzled, I asked myself: do I stand facing the mountain-view hole or facing the door; both positions seemed so very wrong yet each had its logical and compelling reason for being right. One thing for sure, squatting was going to be required, very deep squatting. There was a lovely although smelly hole situated between the two foot markers, dug I presume for the very purpose I was there for, and somewhat familiar as I have used an outhouse before.

Holding my bag firmly in my teeth, clutching my clothing with both hands I squatted the best I could and as you can imagine (but I beg you not to), I was soon in need of toilet paper. It didn't take long to realize there was none to be had. Perhaps there was some in my bag as I pride myself in anticipating these sorts of situations but it might as well have been on the shelf at Wal-Mart as there was no way I could reach it without something touching the floor and for many wet, fragrant, and regrettable reasons, it would not be prudent to let that happen.

Scanning my surroundings I noticed a bucket of water in the corner which I guessed was for "flushing" but do you use the whole bucket or just a little? Or do you pour a small amount on your hand I wondered; yeah like that's possible in my current contortionist position. If you used the whole bucket would people who peed there the rest of the day be without? Would I be the subject of African conversation for weeks to come, "the stupid American used the whole damn bucket of water; what was she thinking?" Is it possible that you would dip your hand in the bucket and then....oh gosh no, that couldn't be right! And why aren't there instructions written on the wall in several languages? This isn't like riding a bike for gosh sakes. Then I see it, a sliver of tissue sticking out from the side of my purse; but how do I reach it? Let's just say; something got wet; something always seems to end up getting wet, doesn't it?

This was my virgin experience with a toilet unlike our American toilet but whether it was a bidet in Europe (what are those prissy things for anyway?!) or a squat toilet in China, I have realized over the years that we are blessed to have indoor plumbing, a toilet that flushes, and the modern facilities we do. I feel like kissing the American toilet every time I return home.

Lost in Translation

When language barriers exist, there is always the potential for misunderstanding. Some misunderstandings can be critical and have consequences; some just turn out to be quite humorous. Such was the case when a friend greeted me at Ataturk Airport in Istanbul, Turkey and excitedly announced his plans for a little road trip.

Friend: "We're not going to stay in Istanbul this weekend; we're going to drive north instead."

"Great", I replied. "Where are we going?"

Friend: "We're going to Biloxi", he proudly exclaimed.

"Wow, that's wonderful", I said. "You know we have a Biloxi in the United States."

Friend: "Really?!"

"Yes, really", I replied.

We drove along through the countryside for about an hour, stopping at a roadside restaurant where we sat outside and enjoyed a lamb dinner grilled tableside by our host, a friend of my companion.

Back on the road, I began asking more questions about our destination. "Is there water in Biloxi?" I asked.

With a very puzzled look on his face, he forced a "Yes" reply. "Yes, there is water in Biloxi."

"Great" I said.

We arrive in a small town situated on the ocean and drive to an area on a cliff overlooking the water just in time to enjoy watching the sunset. It was stunning.

"So what is the name of this body of water?" I ask.
Lightly shaking his head in an "I don't believe you're asking me this again" look, he proclaimed, "BLOCK SEE".

"Oh, it's the Black Sea!" I finally understood.

I thought back to the questions I proposed to him when we were driving. He must have thought I was crazy asking if there was water in BLOCK SEE!

Zenkov Cathredral - Kazakhstan

What's for dinner in Kazakhstan?

World in a Weekend: Kazakhstan

Arriving in the middle of the night at the fog-encrusted airport nearly half a world from home, the whole idea of traveling to Kazakhstan for the weekend seemed quite ridiculous; oh let's face it, it was ridiculous. First an eight hour flight to Frankfurt then another six hour flight to Almaty, Kazakhstan; who in their right mind would do this....intentionally?! Where the heck is Kazakhstan anyway? But here we were twelve time zones from origin and wondering what we were in for. This state of mind continued as my friend and I avoided getting separated and made our way through a sea of a predominantly male black-attired crowd in the arrival area. Fortunately our hotel had sent a shuttle and the driver was there holding a sign when we cleared immigration and customs, reassurance that at least we didn't have to navigate transport at this late hour in a very foreign place and bed was only a shuttle bus ride away.

Our base for the next 24 hours (2am to 2am) was the Intercontinental Almaty hotel which we secured with points, avoiding the $400 plus room rate for this five-star hotel. Almaty, drawing oil industry personnel can be a very expensive city so this was our first cost-cutting measure. Our inability to sleep once at the hotel led us to the lounge where a glass of wine was around $15 and $10 for a beer. This was the cheap end of the scale as it was $10 for a dish of ice cream. Venture outside the hotel and prices are much less of course.

The first morning we woke to a foggy landscape but the snowcapped mountains could be faintly seen in the distant backdrop of the tall shiny skyscrapers. One giant smokestack released a tall stream into the cold Almaty air. It was the only evidence of movement in the stillness of the frosty morning.

A warm breakfast and we headed out on foot to explore the city. We gained a great deal of comfort with our English map in hand but this confidence dwindled when we found that the street signs were only in the local language. It didn't take long to get lost but it took a while before we secured any useable directions in English. We saw the large shiny skyscrapers up close and personal then returned to the hotel to regroup and secure a taxi to the originally intended destination...the Green Bazaar. Not sure what we would find there but it sounded interesting enough and it was near an ornate cathedral I didn't want to miss. A twenty minute cab ride was the equivalent of $7, a fair price to get across town.

The Green Bazaar was a gem of a local market where Kazakhstanis can find anything they would need on a daily basis: kind of a flea market meets farmers market. If you needed fresh sheep's head, they've got it, a thick slice of horse steak, no problem, cheese curds, coming right up. Want something pickled, just name it, it's there. Pickled rooster combs on your shopping list? There's a variety here so don't settle for mundane; the ones with the hot peppers looked very tempting. If you had cabbage on your shopping list, this was your lucky day, they were the size of basketballs or bigger, cheese balls, cheese cubes, cheese crumbles, cheese curds, fresh cream, and every fruit that could be dried (especially apricots!) and free samples! There were dozens of varieties of caviar, salmon, sausages, and smoked meats and fish. The meat area was organized by the types of animal; you have your horse section, your sheep section, your cow section, your pig section and the I-don't-know-what-kind-of-meat-that-is-section. Next door there were hundreds of vendors selling everything from socks to kitchen clocks. I must admit I had thought that this part of the world still suffered from food rations, long lines, and shortages of daily supplies. I am relieved to know there are such grand resources. There were no McDonalds, Starbucks or Kentucky Fried Chicken; but we did see one Pizza Hut, so it appeared that living in Kazakhstan would require a diet of sheep's head and pizza, my observation could be wrong.

Across from the Green Bazaar is Panfilov Park with its stunning war memorials and the magnificent Zenkov Cathedral, the largest wooden cathedral in the world and totally fairy-tale looking. It was Saturday and the locals were out walking with their families and participating in activities that many families in the world do on a sunny Saturday afternoon: feeding pigeons, buying balloons, crying because mom won't buy you snacks, and people watching; the world's favorite sport.

A long walk back to the hotel provided us with additional opportunities to view the local architecture, get a real sense of the city, and take it all in.

While traveling to Kazakhstan in a weekend may seem extreme to most people, I'm glad we went and that we had the opportunity to do it cheaply. This is what seeing the world in a weekend is about.

World in a Weekend: Berlin, Germany

Whether you're a history buff or not, when you visit Berlin you become immersed in it from the time you arrive. The remains of bombed-out buildings still stand, stories and photos of the historical events are preserved at every turn, and you find yourself constantly trying to grasp the reality of what it must have been like living through those times. When my friend suggested Berlin as a weekend jaunt, I thought it was a good choice but I didn't realize the impact such a visit would have.

We chose a convenient and affordable Holiday Inn Express right in the heart of the city, making it easy to explore the area and also have a breakfast for free.

We venture out the first day in the direction of Potsdamer Platz and are greeted with an unexpected surprise, a Christmas market. We had thought it too early for such a treat but we were happy to partake in warm crepes, local sausages and cheese. Large gingerbread hearts hang from the wooden huts and locals drinking mulled wines huddled together. Thousands of sparkling lights and lively music created a festive holiday atmosphere. To top it off, a snow slide had been constructed for tubing right there in the plaza. With our tummies full and warmed and our spirits lifted high, we then moved on in the direction of Brandenburg Gate. We stopped on our way to visit a controversial, but extremely moving memorial, Peter Eisenman's "Monument to the Murdered Jews of Europe". This orchestrated maze of grey geometric cement pillars aligned to allow passage or to sit and reflect is a must-see. We took the time to walk amongst the cobblestone paths and meander between the columns just taking it all in and remembering why it was there. The site is open 24 hours a day allowing easy access for everyone to experience the memorial.

Our day continued with a visit to the Brandenburg Gate where we stood in awe reflecting on the history that took place in this plaza. We followed the Unten den Linden passing historic buildings and museums, portions of the old wall and onwards to Checkpoint Charlie where we resisted having our pictures taken with the Russian and U.S. soldiers (actors) who stand guard between the former

East and West sectors. We do however find other sufficient photo opportunities. My friend now announces he has a surprise in store so we continue on with my curiosity running rampant. He must show me the giant staircase at the Westin Grand made famous in the Bourne Supremacy movie. I'm impressed! We then wander the high end shopping street of Friedrichstrasse partaking in some serious window shopping, eventually bringing us back to our hotel.

After dinner and a good night's sleep we venture out to Alexanderplatz, an area mostly destroyed in World War II that has been renovated and born anew. With bountiful outdoor cafes, charming boutique shops, and a landscaped riverside for strolling, we enjoyed exploring the area and viewing its beautiful old churches. The Berlin TV Tower is located here and offers the highest view in all of Berlin. The line however is much too long so we continue our exploration along the river. We take advantage of endless photo opportunities and walk until we can walk no more. One last stop however before the sun sets, we stop at Topography of Terror, an outdoor exhibit of the former SS bunkers. The narratives and photos were striking and certainly deserving of more than the short hour we spent reading and viewing them.

Since we have purchased a day pass on the train system (about $5.00) we are able to zip around the city and see a great deal more before the evening ended. We were also able to revisit sites at night that we had seen during the day only now they were beautifully lit and appeared even grander.

I left Berlin feeling I had seen and learned so much. However, I knew I had missed a great deal having been there for little more than a day, so this city goes on my list as one to which I must return.

El Zocalo – Mexico City

Photo courtesy of CU Photos

World in a Weekend - Mexico City

We were tired of paying top dollar to go out on New Year's Eve so we thought we had a great idea: bypass the usual spots (Vegas, or the local top restaurant) and consider someplace new. Perhaps a city that has inexpensive lodging, is easy to get to, a vibrant culture and one where the dollar is strong.   Months prior to the holiday we started searching and found a great airfare deal to Mexico City and much to our surprise, a central hotel we could secure with hotel points, making it even a better deal. We were excited.

We arrived to find our hotel in the perfect location, just as we planned. The weather was beautiful so on New Year's Eve we purchased a two day pass for the hop on-hop off bus and secured our transportation for the next two days for less than $20 each. We spent hours over the two-day period traveling from place to place making it an affordable choice for getting around the huge city.

Our hotel was located only a few blocks from the heart of Mexico City, EL Zocalo. We were quite proud of ourselves for selecting such a perfect location. In the afternoon the square was full of locals with their families enjoying the markets and local foods cooked alfresco in the city center. A skating rink was constructed, an annual attraction, and families were enjoying the festivities leading up to the big New Year's celebration.....or so we thought.

Wandering back to our hotel after a day of touring the city we anticipated an exciting evening of fun in the Zocalo and how convenient, only walking distance from the hotel. Ready for a night on the town, we left our hotel room around 9pm. Imagine our surprise when we exited our hotel and found all of the businesses closed! This included all bars/restaurants and retail businesses. The family barbeques were still going strong however and there were police around so we proceeded to ask them where we could possibly find a place to celebrate. After several consultations with each other, they escorted us to a Seven Eleven several blocks away. Confused by the situation, but happy to have even meager libations, we purchase a couple canned vodka drinks and went back to the hotel for drinks and crackers on the roof. We pleaded with the hotel staff to find us an open restaurant but after several calls on our behalf, none were to be found. This is when we discovered our blatant error. It appears that New Year's Eve in Mexico City and perhaps all over Mexico is an at-home family celebration and not a party night like in the U.S. Hence the easily attained, cheap hotel rooms in the center of the city and the huge family barbeques nearby. So the only options in town were private events that we had no access to, or the gigantic family barbeque. Back to EL Zocalo we went, foraging for food. The selections were varied, we found grilled chicken's feet, crickets, fried plantains, baked yams with your choice of toppings, cotton candy, churros, and other local special holiday treats. At midnight the bells in the historic chapels were rung and our New Year's Eve in Mexico City was just fine.

Fortunately New Year's Eve day was one big celebration and we found more than our share of opportunities to celebrate; we were just a day off.

Mexico City is a great city with a lot of depth; there are great discoveries around every corner and more to see than a weekend visit can possibly do justice. If you're going there to celebrate New Year's Eve however, make sure you stay an extra day!

You've arrived at the Equator

World in a Weekend Quito, Ecuador – Center of the World

By now you know that I will go anywhere on a weekend if the price is right and the chance of being murdered is low. Not only was the price right, but Ecuador was a place I had been yearning to explore and the crime rate has become "acceptable world standards" according to Wikipedia. Quito, Ecuador's second largest city has an average year-round temperature of 66 degrees and it is only an hour time difference from Michigan (my home state). Therefore, jet lag is nearly non-existent. The perfect choice for a weekend jaunt!

After I secured my cheap flight and a nearly free stay at a centrally located hotel, I was off to Ecuador. The late arrival left no time for anything but sleep. The morning brought the opportunity for breakfast in the old city. Quito is my kind of place-for just over two bucks I was served a full morning meal of a ham and cheese omelet, a large glass of fresh squeezed mango juice, European pressed coffee, and croissant with butter. Even better, the taxi ride was only one US dollar. Yes, they even use our currency! No worrying about exchange rates here.

You could spend endless hours wandering the cobblestone streets of Quito, photographing the amazing ancient churches (nearly three dozen in the old city), gazing at the mountains in the background, and listening to live music in the squares. I chose to take the cable car to the top of the mountain for a better perspective of the area as a whole.

Altitude adjustment can be a challenge on a short stay with symptoms ranging from a queasy stomach and light-headedness, to shortness of breath from walking up and down the rolling streets. My plan to offset these side-effects was to venture even higher because I know that mountain climbers often ascend to higher altitudes then descend to spend the night to help them acclimate. In reality, I learned that this technique has one major flaw-you have to survive feeling like crap at the higher altitude in order to eventually feel better. I stood only minutes on the 12,000-foot peak, but the views were spectacular.

Additional altitude torture included venturing to the top of a lesser mountain to visit a giant religious virgin statue (as opposed to a non-virgin statue) that overlooks the vast city. This large city has everything with its great outdoor markets, energetic nightlife, and all the upscale amenities you'd expect. What sets Quito apart is the cost to participate; it's all affordable.

When you're only spending a day or two in a city, a tour can be necessary. What do two Japanese, two New Zealanders, a Mexican and an American have in common? More than you would think, as I discovered on our tour. We ventured out to the equator to try our hand at some center-of-the-world experiments and to see what else can happen on a four-hour tour. We first partook in all of the customary things you do on the equator: balanced an egg on the head of a nail, demonstrated how little physical balance you have when trying to walk the equator with your eyes closed, divided our bodies between two hemispheres, took pictures at the zero degree longitude sign, and drank beer. It was the last experiment that led to diversion and to subsequently join in a local celebration of music, dancing and drinking.

When hunger set in, we naturally ordered an array of foods none of us had eaten before including some local favorites: gazpacho with popcorn, roasted guinea pig, and some kind of wonderful spicy cheese and egg soup. Soon, it was obvious that the tour has been extended well beyond its intended four hours. Time does fly by when you're having fun with friends, even new-found ones.

Even in a weekend you can get a taste of another culture and decide if you want to return someday for a bigger bite. Don't be afraid to challenge yourself to a weekend in a foreign country if the price is right and the area is reasonably safe. Remember, the best deals are found when you don't predetermine where you're going. Surprise yourself.

Entering a Market in Ecuador

Sultanamet – The Old City

Photo courtesy of CU Photos

World in a Weekend Istanbul

The most appropriate place to spend Thanksgiving is probably where your family is located. However, if you scored an impossible-to-resist airfare to Istanbul, Turkey, you may have to break the news that you will not be attending this year's family Thanksgiving dinner. Such is the path I chose when I decided to spend Thanksgiving abroad.

Drafting a partner in crime was easy; I found a friend who was up for the trip. Istanbul is the perfect mix of culture, history, night life, grand cuisine, and most of all: affordability. Who wouldn't want to share in a European getaway where you experience the best of Europe without Euro-inflated prices! The dollar is still relatively strong against the Turkish Lira so indulging is easy and affordable.

My favorite part of Istanbul is Sultanahmet, the old town. Surrounded by the wall of Constantinople, it is easily explored on foot or by utilizing the simply designed public transportation grid, perfect when your allotted time for exploring is limited. For the equivalent of a dollar you can ride from one end of the city to the other. Sultanahmet alone hosts enough mosques, cisterns, palaces, ruins, shops and markets to keep you busy for weeks but if you cross over the Galata Bridge you will have a whole new section of the city to explore. Cross the Bosphorus strait by an easily accessed ferry and you enter even another area of the city located in Asia!

Highlights of the city we were able to explore in our weekend included:

The Blue Mosque

The Underground Roman Cisterns

The Grand Bazaar (over 4000 shops!)

The Galata Tower

The Funicular and Tram System

The Egyptian Spice Market

Taksim Shopping District

A Turkish Feast

A Turkish Hamam (bath)

Turkish Sweet Shops

Various Street Markets

The city is like none you have ever visited, both visually stunning, experientially fascinating and a contrast of lifestyles. You can shop the modern streets lined with designer brands or wander markets that date back thousands of years. Search for a new pair of boots or a magic lantern, it's all there. The beautiful sound of the call to prayer may wake you in the morning, while the rocking sounds of club nightlife may keep you awake at night. New tastes are abundant from the endless varieties of Turkish sweets to the exotic spices used in their traditional dishes. Where else in the world could you try ninety different eggplant dishes?! The ornate tiles that cover the large domes of the mosque will amaze you as much as the simple symbol of the evil eye, prominent on everything from jewelry to tea glasses. Istanbul has something for everyone; both vibrant and new, exotic and old.

Ending the trip by relaxing on the hot marble of a Turkish Hamam (it's the local way to unwind), I realize that I can never get enough of Istanbul. I return again and again in an effort to learn more and experience more. It is one of very few cities that call me back on my World in a Weekend ventures.

Where will your World in a Weekend adventure take you?

Istanbul Mosque – Photo courtesy of CU Photos

Taking notes on the Great Wall of China

World in a Weekend Beijing, China

Today I am the luckiest girl in the world as I am writing this while sitting on the steps of the Great Wall of China. I hadn't planned to be here however through a twist of fate, a sale fare, and the fact that I needed to use up an airline voucher expiring at the end of July, here I am. Hearing about the pre-Olympic deals in Beijing, I decided to make this my destination.

Beijing is getting ready for the Olympics and what I've seen of the city thus far is a group of people working extremely hard to be welcoming and helpful. Last night when I arrived, the Olympic greeters were in full force at the airport and most willing to practice their hospitality skills on us non-Olympic folks. They are a kind lot and certainly eager to please but their understanding of simple questions like "where can I get a taxi?" or "where is the exit?" was lacking. But then, I didn't take the time to learn any Chinese before I came here either. Patience, Christine.

My day in Beijing began by arranging transportation to the Great Wall. Options are limited so I sign up for a tour. Then to breakfast which consisted of shrimp and cabbage dumplings, wonderful coffee, bacon, brie, Gouda, salad of fresh greens and figs, just like breakfast at home. Prior to the tour departure I have a couple hours to explore the area around the hotel and discover a flower, fish, and decor market; what a delightful find. I wander the stalls and select a few unique items I cannot buy at home: a fish-shaped business card holder, a colorful apron, and fake dragon flies. You can never have enough fake dragon flies. There are hundreds of orchids, exotic plants, bonsai, and an assortment of colorful fish. On my way back to the hotel I walk past the U.S. Embassy. It is being completely remodeled. A fortified compound, I decide it is not a place to linger but manage to snap a couple pictures when the guards weren't looking.

Back at the hotel, I catch my bus and I am off to the Great Wall. I chose the Mutianyu section of the wall because it is less touristy and it offers cable car transportation to the top. It is 95 degrees and I would like to spend my energy walking up and down the Great Wall not just to reach it. Many people are weak and overheated just hiking to the cable car station. The sun is blistering but I count my blessings as I was told this past week has been foggy and this is the first clear day. I was very lucky that my cable car to the top was the same exact car that President Clinton took to the top when he came to the Great Wall; this information was posted inside the car! Ok, I can't help thinking, my butt sat where his butt sat. But then I thought I might be sitting in the wrong place so I made sure I sat in every area of the car. Now I can say that I sat where he sat.

The Wall is an amazing sight, meandering through the mountains; you can even see Mongolia from here! I take many pictures, hike up and down the endless steps, rest to write part of this article and enjoy my time on the wall. I reflect in awe as to how such a wall could be built by human hands. Well, it *is* one of the Seven Wonders of the World.

My precious hours on the Great Wall have come to an end and after a lovely ride through the forests and agricultural areas; we are back in the city. I have a lovely dinner of local cuisine and get a good night's sleep before heading to the airport. My visit was short but I know I will return to Beijing. It is a great value for your travel dollar and it delivers a unique and positive cultural experience.

Beijing Flower Market

Street sign north of Bogota'

World in a Weekend Bogota, Colombia

I've always wanted to go to Colombia. I've heard it was beautiful although dangerous but lately the reports have been much more positive. Add the fact that I found a cheap airfare and it really wasn't a difficult decision to go.

Excited, but a little nervous about my decision to go *"alone"* (no one I knew would even consider going with me), I find myself packing for my weekend trip to Bogotá. I couldn't help thinking as I'm packing, "are these the shoes I could wear for five years in captivity?" I threw in a more

77

comfortable pair. In the not too distant past, kidnapping and drug-related crime activities were commonplace in Colombia. Now this activity is all but history in the urban areas and visiting is as safe as any major city. As an extra precaution, I select a hotel in the safest area of the city versus more traditional lodging outside the city center.

Arriving late at night, I rely on a couple of friendly locals to assist me in navigating the taxi line process. A ticket here, money exchange there, and describing where I needed to go went smoothly with their help. Flat rate versus a meter; I liked that. I may get kidnapped but I certainly won't get ripped off by the taxi driver. Riding to my hotel late at night, no matter which foreign city I'm in, I usually mumble to myself, (as I do once again tonight), "WHAT AM I DOING HERE?" I know however that morning *always* answers that question.

Taxi to the hotel: 20 million pesos ($9), glass of wine in the hotel lobby after getting settled $3, bedtime in Bogotá.....heavenly.

Ah, Saturday morning and the sky is clear. Bogotá has a year-round average temperature of about sixty degrees. This is the rainy season so I am happy to see the sun. I ask at the front desk for input as to what I should see and do in Bogotá and soon I am surrounded by helpful people offering their favorites. It is unanimous that I must go to Zipaquira, the underground salt cathedrals. Nothing like it in the world, they say. Oh she must go to Andreas; you can't miss Andreas (a popular eating venue) when you're in Bogotá. Oh and you have to see Cajica (a nearby town) and Monseratte (the mountains). I decide to try to see them all.

It is recommended that I not travel alone so the hotel arranges a driver. My driver (secured for $8 an hour) speaks *some* English. I tell him "today I will learn more Spanish and you will learn more English". We laugh. Bogotá is beautiful, the weather perfect, and the people incredibly kind. I enjoy my ride to the countryside and the underground Cathedrals in the salt mines. I have a delicious lunch experience with my driver at Andreas where everything is a crazy-wonderful, artsy, meat infested circus: way too unique to describe. I visit some antique shops, walk around a small town, ride through the mountains, and as the sun goes down I return to my hotel to regroup.

Evening is special; the streets are alive and vibrant with Latin music. The area around the main park is concentrated with salsa bars, restaurants, and cafes. The ladies look their best, dressed up for their Saturday night out to let everyone know the night is a special one for them. The men take notice and the fun begins. I enjoy a glass of sangria, conversation with other travelers, people watching, and listening to the live music; this rounds out my evening just fine. You can't help but enjoy yourself on a night out in the streets of Bogotá, its electric.

Alas my day in Bogotá is ending but it was a very good one. I couldn't have been more comfortable and more exhilarated at the same time. I have a list of activities I want to experience when I return.....and I will return. Next time however, I'll pack the *fancy* shoes!

Entrance to Salt Cathedrals – Bogota'

Old Shanghai

World in a Weekend Shanghai

I read an article a couple years ago that contained a list of ten places to see in the next five years because they were vanishing. I remember one was the snows of Kilimanjaro, and another was Old Shanghai. I don't remember the other eight on the list, but when my friend called and asked me to go to Shanghai for the weekend as he had found a great airfare, I remembered the list and said yes. Why go to China for a weekend? Why not?!

It was an eleven hour flight to Tokyo and just 2-3 additional hours on to Shanghai. The flight went quickly as we caught up on each other's lives. We land right on time and because we had the foresight to ask the flight attendant to write the name and address of our hotel in Chinese for our taxi driver, we arrive easily at our hotel. We take time to relax and get a good night's sleep for our full day tomorrow.

We wake refreshed and head directly to Old Shanghai. We discover that since taxi rides are only $2-5 wherever we chose to go, we will have no problem maximizing our time here and doing it inexpensively. We continue to explore the temples and endless shopping in Old Shanghai, and then wander the streets in the adjoining neighborhoods. The streets are filled with shops where the locals buy household goods. Each shop is a specialty store carrying basically one type of item such as paper products, furniture, baked goods, underwear, or any household item one would need. We discover beautiful parks with endless varieties of trees and plants. Some sidewalks are lined with blooming cherry trees, others not so pretty or pleasantly fragrant but each one a cultural surprise.

We wander until we reach the Bund, a waterfront boardwalk about two miles long. From there we view the amazing architecture of Shanghai. The buildings are so colorful and beautifully designed they remind me of a garden; a garden of buildings that pleased the eye as much as a garden of flowers. The waterway was just as colorful with even the most mundane coal barge painted green, gold, and orange and the tour boats with their dragon facades and temple-like appearance burst with more shades of red than I thought possible. We continue on to Shanghai's famous shopping street, Nanjing road where it's an effort to keep from turning this exploration into a shopping trip. It seems like we have been here for days, and it's only lunchtime.

Speaking of lunchtime; it was time to find a place to eat. We take a chance on a traditional place, packed with locals and very inviting. We are rewarded with a spread of delicious chicken and pork dishes and super-sized beers for two thirsty wanderers for a total of $7. Our tummies full we decide to head back to the hotel and rest up a bit before our evening excursion. After a brief nap we head to the lower level of the hotel and take in some bowling (yes, bowling). We bowl a few games, laughing at our circumstance of having our own private bowling alley in a hotel basement in Shanghai.

Back to the Bund (boardwalk) we venture to view the garden of buildings at night. We walk the Bund and are not disappointed by the display. We also wander over once again to Nanjing Road; picture Times Square multiplied ten times and more exotic as the signs are in Chinese; a generous feast for the senses.

It's time to head back to the hotel, get a good night's sleep, and pack for the trip home. Our day in Shanghai was extraordinary and certainly resonated as a destination worth a return trip.

My expectations of China, prior to us arriving, were to be followed and watched, to experience red tape and bureaucracy, to find people repressed and not enjoying life. While I'm sure there are consequences for not conforming, I found a warm, caring, expressive, energized group of (by the way), very fashionable people, living and working peacefully, some even eager to share their opinions on the safe ear of a foreigner. While we did see a lot of security personnel, we never felt like we were under surveillance or that we couldn't go where we wanted to go when we wanted to go there. This is just my limited view in my one day in Shanghai, but what a day it was. Why go to China for the weekend? Why not?! Was it worth the trip? Oh yes, it was.

Barbican Castle

Photo courtesy of CU Photos

World in a Weekend Warsaw Poland

Airfares are increasing and finding a bargain fare to Europe is becoming difficult. I've recently had to resort to foreign lesser-known airlines to score some of the deals I was once able to find with our domestic brands. One of these foreign airlines is LOT, the Polish airline. Every Wednesday LOT offers 30% off fares and occasionally you can book a flight to Poland for $300-$400 from Chicago. Remember my mantra; the destination is not predetermined so we will go where LOT goes, in this case: Warsaw.

The gate agent for LOT has some great travel advice for us: "You should not go to Warsaw; it is boring, I do not like it. I like Krakow; you should go to Krakow". Why thank you for your recommendation Ms. Gate Agent as we check in for our Warsaw flight; it's always good to receive travel advice that confirms our stupidity for choosing the entirely wrong city to visit. This is where our Polish experience began and subsequently escalated. As we made our way to the gate, we soon realized we had entered the Polish zone without possessing the necessary language skills we needed to survive in that section of the airport. Worse yet, in appearance we could have passed for Polish citizens so everyone spoke to us only in Polish. We did a lot of nodding our heads and smiling and then boarded the plane when we felt like it because we had no clue as to what was going on. Hours later, after watching a few Polish cartoons and music videos, dining on a couple meals of peas and carrots, and experiencing being cramped in seats smaller and less comfortable than grade school auditorium bleachers, we were in Poland.

It was a cold winter day in the capital city of Warsaw yet our spirits were high and we were anxious to explore this historic city. Warsaw is historic for a lot of reasons including the fact that it was 85% destroyed by the Nazis in World War II but has since been rebuilt. The best part of the rebuilt city is the Old Town as it captures the look and feel of the original city. It really does look as old as it should be if it hadn't been nearly completely destroyed. It has mostly original cobblestone streets, inviting shops, art galleries, restaurants, bars, entertainment and lots of pigeons. It also has hot beer, pierogies, and pazckis, all of which we planned to sample. My friend has her own personal quest to seek out a certain brand of bison grass vodka which I'm hopeful we'll be able to find but if not, a vodka search alone sounds like a worthy endeavor.

That was day one. Grant you, there are hundreds of great buildings in Warsaw and we saw nearly all of them the first day. The second day we saw the rest. Walking nearly 15 miles over the two days (my friend had a pedometer for gosh sakes) we became intimate with every significant piece of architecture, every park, and every street in Warsaw that we couldn't pronounce. We found and drank their bison grass vodka and their hot beer (highly recommended), we ate their fresh pazckis, their sausages, and their pierogies, and we enjoyed the friendliness of the Polish people. We searched in vain for a good polka band but settled happily for an elderly man playing the accordion on a street corner, a young gal yelling Sinead O'Connor songs in an alley, and a mime in the metro tunnel.

It was a fun weekend and a successful vodka search but would I return to Poland? Of course, they all knew how to pronounce my name. Next time however, I plan to visit Krakow.

Panama Canal

World in a Weekend Panama City

Now here's a place to check out: Panama City. Not Panama City, Florida but Panama City, Panama. All the fresh seafood you can eat, beautiful beaches, a happening night life, great shopping, arts and culture, historically fascinating, affordable medical and dental care, and home of the Panama Canal. Although nearly in South America, Panama is only a four-hour flight from Atlanta, Georgia.

Arriving about 10pm on a Friday night, the city looked huge. Was I in for anything more than a hot, humid weekend in a crowded city; thankfully not. Saturday morning I was able to secure an excellent deal on an English speaking driver who would be my companion for the next 9 hours. At $50 it was a bargain and he even returned to the hotel to pick up my friend who arrived later in the day, no extra charge.

You can learn a lot about an area in a day; especially when you have a willing driver who answers any questions you pose. I like to learn the economics of the average citizen and he was willing to share all. "How much would that house cost, how much does it cost to buy a car, how much is electricity, how much is internet?" I'm usually full of economic questions and my driver shared all he knew. One thing for sure, Panama is booming. There are new developments everywhere and even the old city has renovation fever. Its fabulous colonial buildings are being transformed into quaint shops, apartments, and fine restaurant and cafes. Many Americans, Columbians, and Europeans retire here and invest here. International Living Magazine (www.interantionalliving.com) praises it as having an array of perks for retirees and a process for Americans to become residents that is second to none.

I visited the ruins of the early settlements, the rain forest preserve, and the seafood market where an entire grilled lobster dinner with wine could be had for less than twenty dollars. All my meals were fresh seafood as I couldn't resist inexpensive seafood fresh from the ocean! With a full stomach, it was off to visit the Panama Canal. We spent a couple hours there and watched the ships pass slowly through the locks. As one of the marvels of the modern world, it's a sight you should experience in your lifetime. It's not just seeing the canal; it's learning the story behind its creation that is even more fascinating.

The currency used in Panama is the American Dollar, no money exchange worries here. Many people speak English and if they don't, they are used to dealing with Americans and are very patient. Menus and signs are in Spanish and English so you will have no trouble ordering meals and getting around. Prices are also very reasonable. And speaking of prices, the shopping is fabulous. I scored some "designer" sunglasses for $4, a cotton hand-beaded top for $6 and a pound of Panamanian coffee for $3. If I had more time, I'd have done some serious damage working my way up to the real designer labels.

An evening of incredible salsa music, a few rum and cokes, a visit to the casino, and hanging out at the local pub accounted for my Saturday night in Panama. I will return to discover more about this city; this just wasn't enough.

Istanbul Street at Night – Photo Courtesy of CU Photos

Old City – Quito, Ecuador

Famous Jumbo Restaurant – Aberdeen, Hong Kong

World in a Weekend Hong Kong

When you find a good fare, you have to share. Such was the case when I invited two friends (separately) to go to Hong Kong and to my surprise they both accepted. So off we went for a weekend in Hong Kong. I have visited many times since 1995 and each visit has been met with extraordinary changes in the city. No longer are the city streets lined with small businesses and Chinese charm as high-rise buildings and elevated highways now monopolize this landscape of expensive real estate. However, Hong Kong and its sister Kowloon still retain their uniqueness and beg you to dig beneath the modern surface to find your own special hidden Chinese treasures.

The enchanting bird market where Chinese men walk their caged birds, sharing their songs with other caged and wild birds in the area, is still there. The night markets, temples, flower market, Victoria Peak, Stanley and its renown marketplace, the giant Buddha, and numerous other famous Hong Kong and area sites are also still there, you just have to seek them out amongst the new modern façade.

Since this is my friend's first time here, he entrusts me to plan the day. We catch a city bus for one of my favorite excursions, the trip to the other side of Hong Kong Island to visit the Stanley Market. It's an hour trip but the bus is comfortable, the views are spectacular and you get to see how the people live and play; best of all, the trip costs around $2 each way. Bargains abound at the market: silk ties for $1.50, cashmere sweater for $15, silk pajamas $7, and silk scarves $2. The market also has a great selection of local art, both traditional and contemporary. Since Stanley's marketplace is located on the water, when you are finished making your purchases, you can relax for a nice lunch at one of the waterside restaurants.

Another favorite activity is to stop off at the fishing town of Aberdeen, located along the bus route, and catch one of the many small fishing vessels to take a tour of the harbor. Stand along the water and wave your hand and soon one of the boat owners will stop and pick you up. Negotiate a fare (in our case a thirty-minute cruise was about $7 a person) and you'll have your own personal tour. On a hot day, which we experienced, being on the water can be a welcome relief from the heat. Since Hong Kong harbors are nearly absent of fish these days, life can be a struggle for the residents in the fishing community. Take into account that they are surrounded by some the most expensive real estate in the world and you can understand some of the challenges they face. The area however still retains the quaint fishing life atmosphere and is a gem you should visit while it is still there. When you're finished with your boat ride, stop by the large and very famous JUMBO floating restaurant, an ornate sight for the eyes and a pleasing experience for the stomach.

Since Hong Kong is surrounded by water, the options for experiencing the city from the water are abundant. One great way to view the city, and also a bargain, is from the deck of the Star Ferry. For around 30 cents you can get a great view of the harbor and the amazing skyline, especially on a voyage taken at dusk when the lights of the city turn on just to amaze you. There is also a Chinese "Junk" boat called Duk Ling which is one of the last remaining traditional junks and tourists can enjoy a ride for a reduced fee. Additionally, there are party boats, dinner cruises, and charters; literally a boat for every timeframe and budget.

Add your own perfect ending to a day in the city by taking in a club, enjoying a quiet cocktail overlooking the harbor, wander through a night market, or head up to the top of Victoria Peak. Then, you've experienced Hong Kong as we did. (Sigh), I think I'm ready to go back.

Free Hula Show - Honolulu

World in a Weekend – Honolulu

Honolulu, Hawaii rocks for a lot of reasons: its famous beaches, that turquoise water, those surfers, the fabulous shopping, superb international cuisine, and its unique culture. While I have visited several times, on this particular trip I brought along a friend who used to live there so I was excited to experience Honolulu in a slightly different way, perhaps a little more local.

The weekend began in the normal fashion: secured a nice Sheraton hotel (with points) near the beach, got upgraded to an ocean view room with breakfast and internet included, and ventured out to walk the beach and mingle among the tourists. This time however, I had my local resource with me who knew which venues had the best free entertainment, the best ocean views, and the best cocktails! It was a nice foundation for a fun weekend in Honolulu.

Our bucket list for Saturday, our only full day in the city, was to seek out a variety of free activities, indulge in a little shopping and above all, attend the 10th Annual Spam Jam Festival. What we didn't anticipate were the interesting people we would meet along the way.

We didn't make it far from our hotel room before noticing a group of Japanese people holding ukuleles in their hands led by what appeared to be an instructor. I asked if I could join and immediately I was taking ukulele lessons. Our master instructor, Daniel Nakashima was a patient and persistent leader who, after less than thirty minutes managed to teach us to play a lovely song. The crowd gathered around us and cheered at our performance. This was a special day for the ukulele in Hawaii because today they would attempt to break the Guinness Book of World Records record for the number of ukulele players (1500) at one sitting. Currently held by Sweden, Hawaii would attempt for a second time to secure the title. Unfortunately we did not attend the event as it conflicted with the Spam Jam but we later learned they fell short of the record, by a couple hundred attendees, better than their 2007 attempt, but not as good as their next attempt where they fully expect to be victorious.

Not far from the site of my ukulele lessons we discovered a hula show and paused to take it all in. Yes, we were in Hawaii, ocean in the background, palm trees blowing in the wind, surfers catching the waves, and the sound of island music in the air. Life is good, very good, another Mai tai please.

While the day was still young and our energy high, my friend suggested we visit some of the grand Waikiki beach hotels. It was a great way to get some walking in and also a way to check out where we might want to stay in the future. We stopped at a hotel where the dining room featured a floor to ceiling aquarium; we were lucky as it was feeding time for the stingrays. We sat on the old veranda of the Moana Surfrider and awed at the old famous banyan tree. We wandered through another historic hotel, The Royal Hawaiian, the pink luxurious classic that has been there since 1927. It was leased by the Navy for the troops R & R during the war; but fortunately it opened again to the public so we can all enjoy its historic beauty. We visited posh gift shops, grand lobbies, and stopped now and then to take in the ocean views and listen to live Hawaiian music.

There was one special shop we visited that will stand out in our memory. The shop was just a nice jewelry store in one of the large hotels but it was the salesperson Mr. Hong who made it so special. Mr. Hong works for Island Jewelry but he is a passionate soul about everything he does, not just selling jewelry. He has perfected a way to cut a Hawaiian mango so it spreads out like a fan and can be easily eaten without having the large pit get in the way. Oh yes, and he has a slide show about the process. Mr. Hong is also an expert on the colored beaches of Hawaii. You have your green sand beach, your red sand beach, black, and then white. He thought it would be a great conversation starter to wear a red, white and blue outfit and stand on the green beach. We thought so too. Mr. Hong is a gracious soul and he proved it my letting us try on two beautiful coral necklaces that had a total value of nearly $25,000! He explained the rarity of coral these days and gave us a little lesson on the different varieties and styles. Mr. Hong was a walking encyclopedia and fascinating to meet. His promise to send me his mango cutting pictures complete with instructions on which mangos to buy and when to buy them, and his slide show of the colored sand beaches was fulfilled when both showed up in my email later that day.

I have a new respect for Honolulu as I get to know more of the people here. I always thought of it as just another big city with a great location (on a beach). This weekend changed my view of the city tremendously. Then we attended the 10th Annual Waikiki Spam Jam.

Hawaii loves Spam. It arrived with the American troops during WWII and has been a part of the local diet ever since. Why so popular? Well, it is certainly a versatile product having a long shelf life, it works well in all types of recipes, it has a nice, salty flavor, and it's affordable. Spam Jam celebrates this special canned meat by presenting the world with a venue for a taste of all things SPAM.

The streets of Waikiki are blocked off from vehicle traffic and the booths and music stages are set up. You'll hear sixties music, reggae, other classic rock and quite frankly any other music that goes with Spam; that would be all music except maybe Beethoven and Nora Jones. The dishes range widely from Spam nachos, Spam sliders, maple Spam pancakes, Spam stir fry and even Spam doughnuts. The most popular concoction may be Spam musubi. It is pronounced MOO-su-bee and it is made like sushi but take my advice and don't call it that. You can find it in convenience stores, gas stations, malls and beaches, and anywhere you'd want a quick bite to eat.

We tried a couple dishes and man, this stuff was good. I'm having a Spam craving right now. Top chefs challenge to make even more sophisticated dishes such as garlic shrimp and Spam skewers and Spam spring rolls.

In addition to the Spam smorgasbord of food booths, you have several local artists and retail vendors selling their wares. The local food bank also utilizes the festival to help seek food donations for the area's less fortunate. Local businesses support the efforts by offering incentives if you bring a food item for donation. All in all Spam Jam is a great affair for everyone.

Having attending Spam Jam and happy we did, we now search for the perfect spot for our last cocktail on the beach before heading back to the hotel room to pack. The sunset is amazing and we select a table with the perfect view. While snapping one last photo of the beach I notice an older couple watching the sunset and drinking Mai tais. I approached them to show how lovely they looked in the photo. The conversation lead to them inviting us over to their table and we spent the evening sharing wonderful stories. They were world travelers from London. He, (a novelist) and his wife were traveling with their professionally accomplished daughter who had some great (and funny) travel stories of her own. How lucky we were to meet such interesting people.

The evening was a perfect ending to a perfect weekend in Honolulu. We grabbed a bottle of Champagne on the way back to our hotel room just to make packing to go home more tolerable.

Decisions in Bonaire

World in a Weekend – Bonaire

I could describe Bonaire as an island known for incredible scuba diving located off the coast of Venezuela in the Dutch Antilles or I could refer to it as one of those odd destinations that popped up with a very cheap airfare during the shoulder season, either would be accurate but the second reference is how I came to book a trip to this island of which I know nothing.

It was Friday and we worked at our day job all day then caught an evening flight towards our Bonaire island getaway. By now, you probably know my theory: sleep in your bed and you will wake up in your bedroom; sleep on a plane and you will wake up (in this case) in Bonaire!

As I stare out the window of the airplane, I can see the island in the distance. It appears to be covered with salt! Well indeed it was as one portion of the island is where the salt company builds pyramids of drying salt; pyramids of rose tinted salt from the sea are my first glimpse of this paradise.

Arriving early in the morning, we have the entire day and evening to discover what this island has to offer. We chose an ocean front room in a funky resort close to the airport and within walking distance to town to make the most of our short time here. Since we're splitting the room cost and we're only here for one night, our costs are kept low. It turns out to be the best oceanfront room ever. When we open our patio door, we find we are literally on the water, the gentle surf slapping against the rocks less than five feet from our deck.

The multi-colored Caribbean themed resort is over the top with character and there is no shortage of activity options. I may be worldly but I do not swim so my snorkeling choice was a leap of faith. It seemed appropriate however with the coral beds right in front of our hotel. So, after a leisurely breakfast overlooking the ocean, we head down to explore the under waters of Bonaire.

I giggled like a little girl as I spotted the colorful variety of fish swimming right past my face. Several times I took in a lot of water, not being familiar with proper snorkeling techniques but eventually I got the hang of it. I eagerly went back for two more snorkeling sessions throughout the day. My friend was swimming circles around me mostly to make sure I was doing okay then she headed out to deeper waters for the real underwater show. Later we were able to share fish sightings by referencing a fish ID book; it was amazing the variety of fish we saw.

The day lingered as we enjoyed the luxury of doing nothing on a beach lounge between snorkeling sessions. Evening brought the opportunity to walk into town and find an eating establishment we could both declare as interesting enough to try. We were thrilled to discover a superb little eatery serving a fresh savory grilled fish dinner, service making you feel like you were a regular and the view I swear I've seen on a postcard. Did I mention the sunset?

The magical day came to a close after enjoying the local beats of a steel drum band and partaking in a few games of chance at the resort's onsite casino.

No we didn't do an island tour, rent a car or even book scuba diving lessons on our World in a Weekend trip to Bonaire, but why mess with perfection?! That is the only word I can use to describe this sip of paradise, perfection. Bonaire, an odd location that popped up on the cheap airfare radar screen and turned out to be one of my most memorable World in a Weekend destinations.

Divi Flamingo Resort - Bonaire

In Closing....

Can you really see the world in a weekend? Not really, from a practical perspective you can only get a glimpse of what is out there, an amazing, inspiring, and motivating glimpse. My hope is that some of my concepts, ideas, and experiences will inspire you to look at your travels differently. Perhaps you'll even consider "throwing away the destination" the next time you plan your annual getaway, a small decision that could push you out of your comfort zone and into the world.

Christine Krzyszton
Travel Writer
"Learn how to see the World in a Weekend"

Vi   see

th

800 Cottageview Dr, Ste 209
Traverse City, MI 49684

czstreet@aol.com

www.frugaltravelguy.com/author/christinekrzyszton

Made in the USA
Charleston, SC
04 October 2013